FEATHERED FRIENDS

EAGLES

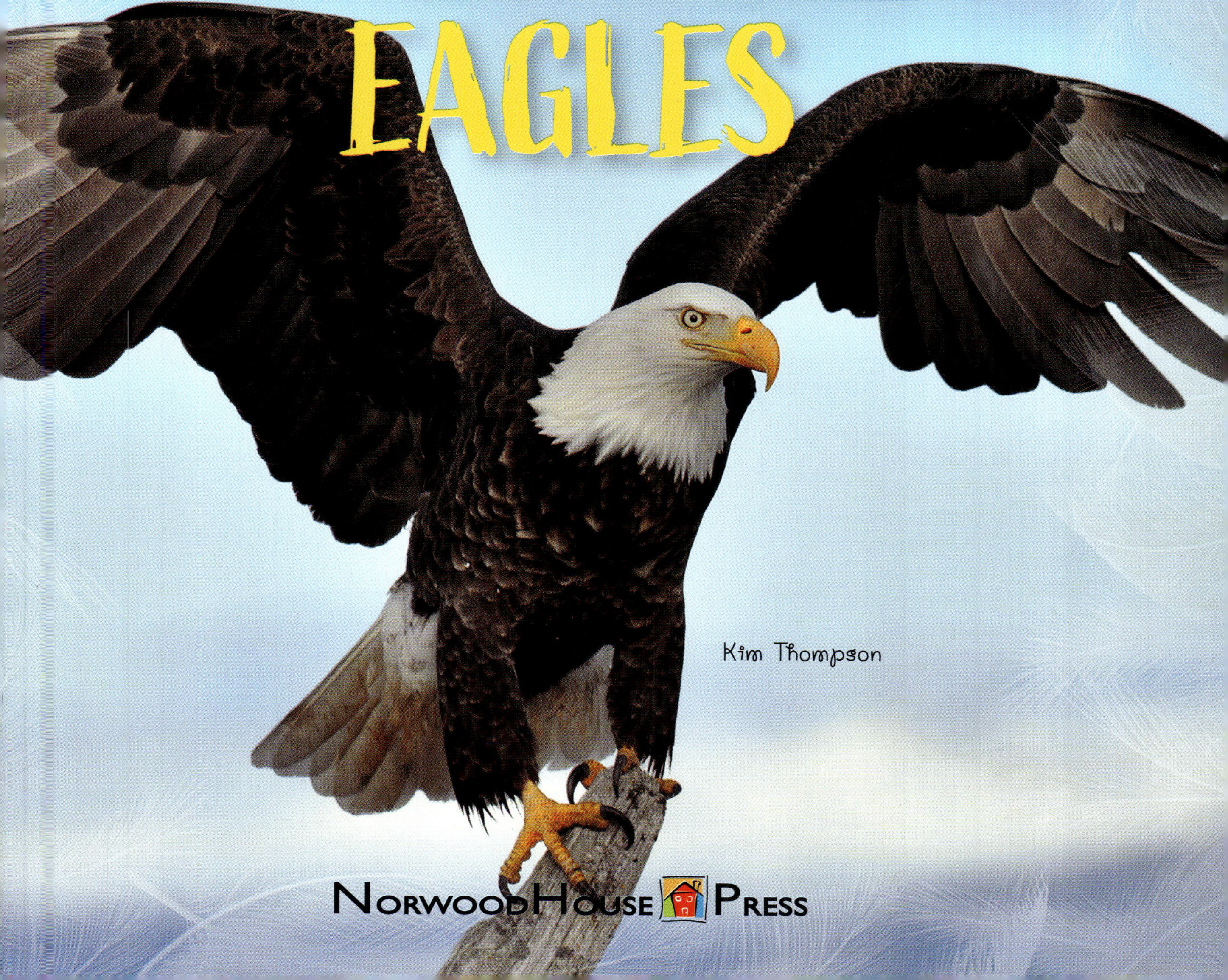

Kim Thompson

NorwoodHouse Press

Cataloging-in-Publication Data

Names: Thompson, Kim.
Title: Eagles / Kim Thompson.
Description: Buffalo, NY : Norwood House Press, 2027. | Series: Feathered friends | Includes glossary and index.
Identifiers: ISBN 9781978580473 (pbk.) | ISBN 9781978580480 (library bound) | ISBN 9781978580497 (ebook)
Subjects: LCSH: Eagles--Juvenile literature. | Eagles--Life cycles--Juvenile literature. | Eagles--Behavior--Juvenile literature.
Classification: LCC QL696.F32 T548 2027 | DDC 598.942--dc23

Published in 2027 by
Norwood House Press
2544 Clinton Street
Buffalo, NY 14224

Designer: Rhea Magaro
Editor: Tricia Hoffman

Photo credits: Cover, p.1 FloridaStock/Shutterstock.com; p.5 Wirestock Creators/Shutterstock.com; p.6 Jerry Bouwmeester/Shutterstock.com; p.8 Aikhan000042/Shutterstock.com; p.9 alberto clemares exposito/Shutterstock.com; p.11 Indra_Wd/Shutterstock.com; p.12 Dennis W Donohue/Shutterstock.com; p.13 wendy blanchard/Shutterstock.com; p.15 Vaclav Matous/Shutterstock.com; p.16 Bryan Eastham/Shutterstock.com; p.19 rustycanuck/Shutterstock.com; p.21 Locomotive74/Shutterstock.com;

Printed in the United States of America

CPSIA compliance information: Batch #CSNHP27: For further information contact Norwood House Press at 1-800-237-9932.

TABLE OF CONTENTS

What Do Eagles Look Like?

Eagles are our feathered friends. They are large birds of prey, or **raptors**. Their **wingspan** can be more than seven feet (two meters). When flying, eagles rarely flap their giant wings. They soar on the wind.

Eagles are built for hunting. They have thick, hooked beaks. At the end of each foot are four sharp, curved claws called **talons**.

There are more than 60 eagle **species**. Each looks a little different from the others. Bald eagles are not really bald. They have brown bodies and white heads.

Golden eagles have golden-brown feathers on their heads and necks.

Where Do Eagles Live?

Eagles live on every continent except Antarctica. They fly over mountains, forests, and fields. Many stay near lakes and rivers where they can catch fish.

Bald eagles and golden eagles live in North America.

How Do Eagles Grow Up?

Mates stay together for life. They use the same nest year after year.

A female bald eagle lays up to three eggs at a time. The male and female take turns keeping the eggs warm. After they hatch, babies stay near the nest for months. Their parents teach them to hunt.

What Do Eagles Eat?

Eagles are **carnivores**. Their **keen** eyes spot **prey** from miles away. They swoop down and grab animals without landing. Then, they fly to a perch where they rip the food apart.

Eagles eat whatever they can catch. They look for fish, snakes, rabbits, foxes, other birds, or even small deer. Eagles also eat roadkill and other **carrion**.

What Sounds Do Eagles Make?

Eagles are not big talkers. They call to give warnings and protect their nests. Babies call to beg for food.

Golden eagles make whistling sounds. Bald eagles make quiet chirps.

What Funny Things Can Eagles Do?

Pairs of bald eagles “cartwheel.” They grip talons high in the sky. They fall down while spinning. Just before hitting the ground, they separate and fly back up.

GLOSSARY

carnivores (KAHR-nuh-vorz): animals that eat meat

carrion (KER-ee-uhn): rotting, dead meat

keen (keen): sharp, quick, or alert; highly developed

prey (pray): animals that are hunted and eaten by other animals

raptors (RAP-turz): large, predatory birds that eat meat or carrion and that have hooked beaks and sharp talons, including hawks, eagles, and owls

species (SPEE-sheez): groups of living things that are alike and can reproduce together

talons (TAL-uhnz): sharp claws of a bird of prey such as an eagle, hawk, or falcon

wingspan (WING-span): the distance between the outer tips of the outstretched wings of a bird

THINKING QUESTIONS

1. What is a bird of prey?
2. How does an eagle's body help it hunt?
3. What eagle species live in North America?
4. What do eagles eat?
5. What is "cartwheeling"?

INDEX

ABOUT THE AUTHOR

Kim Thompson is a writer from Columbus, Ohio. She has written many books for kids. Lots of birds come to her backyard feeder. Her favorites are the showy red cardinals, tiny bright goldfinches, and waddling mallard ducks. Her two cats watch from the window.